BIRDS OF THE WORLD
GAME BIRDS

BIRDS OF THE WORLD
GAME BIRDS

JOHN P.S. MACKENZIE

NorthWord
INC

Originally published in Canada by Key Porter Books Limited, Toronto

Published in the United States by:
NorthWord Press Inc.
Box 1360
Minocqua, Wisconsin
54548

ISBN: 1-55971-043-8

Library of Congress Catalogue Card Number 88-061092

For a free catalog describing NorthWord's books call 1-800-336-5666

Typesetting: Southam Business Information and Communications Group Inc.

Printed and bound in Italy

Page 2: Mourning Dove (*Zenaidura macroura*)   The Mourning Dove usually makes its nest in coniferous trees, but buildings and other trees are also used. In southern areas, the two eggs may be laid in February; later farther north. Three or four broods may be raised each year.

Pages 4-5: Helmeted Guinea Fowl (*Numida mitrata*)   The name "Guinea Fowl" comes from the area of West Africa around the Gulf of Guinea. Domesticated stock originated there. It is gregarious and feeds in flocks.

CONTENTS

INTRODUCTION

Left: Ruddy Pigeon (*Columba subvinacae*) This brown pigeon has a purplish band on the back of the neck. It lives from Costa Rica south to northern Argentina, usually at altitudes above 3,500 feet. It is a forest species, and is usually seen high in the trees.

Ring-necked Pheasant (*Phasianus colchicus*) Large numbers of this species are bred in Europe and North America. They do well in captivity and in the wild, provided sufficient cover and food are available.

The term "game birds" is, to ornithologists, the name applied to all those birds of the order of Galliformes which consists of the families of pheasants, grouse, turkeys, guinea fowl, megapodes and curassows. Most people would, however, think of game birds as all birds that are shot for food or sport. These additional groups would include ducks, geese, doves, pigeons, some of the rails, snipe, woodcock, sandgrouse and, in some countries, even songbirds. In the more developed countries there is little need to shoot birds for food. In some less developed countries, where the supply of protein is scarce, shooting and trapping for food often put great pressure on bird populations. Taking this somewhat wider definition into account, in this volume we shall describe the Galliformes and also include the doves and pigeons, and woodcock and snipe. Both the woodcock and snipe species are part of the sandpiper group which, though not galliform birds, are commonly hunted for food. Sandgrouse are also described.

Birds are sometimes killed for reasons other than sport or food, usually with disastrous results. Some years ago the government of China concluded that birds were having a negative effect on agriculture. Millions of people were sent into the fields and what is left of the forests to beat pans in order to frighten the birds. This was kept up for days until huge numbers died of exhaustion and starvation. Thus, by decree, virtually all birds in agricultural areas were eliminated. It was soon realized that, without birds, insects multiplied unchecked, and it was not long before a now wise government was taking steps to encourage birds. This is, perhaps, an extreme case, but there have been many examples where heavy slaughter has backfired.

Birds of prey are often shot — sometimes in spite, for there is a continuing superstition that they are harmful. It has, however, been generally established that birds of prey help to maintain a proper balance in the populations of animals and birds that are subject to their predation. And most do not eat game birds or waterfowl — those species sought by hunters.

Primates of many sorts, including our ancestors, have doubtless always eaten birds whenever possible. It is not known when humans began to take birds as food, but the drawings in the cave of Lascaux, in France, indicate that they were doing so at least 100,000 years ago. This was during a warm period between the great ice ages after which several of the animals there depicted disappeared from southern Europe. Evidence remaining in Stone Age caves indicates that the preference was for mammals killed with darts and throwing sticks. The bow and arrow were used starting about 70,000 years ago, and it subsequently became possible to take birds as well.

People learned that some birds are more pleasing to eat than others. As a consequence, they concentrated on the more edible species, neglecting strong flavored ones such as loons, shelduck and scoters. In the developed regions of the world the number of wild birds eaten is very small. The fact is, if every person in the world were to start eating wild birds, the total supply would last about one day.

Of course, a vast quantity of the flesh of domesticated birds is eaten. The birds we eat have been domesticated in India for more than 4,000 years and, in China, for more than 3,000 years. In 1520 Cortez introduced chickens into Mexico. Four years later turkeys from North America were taken to Europe. The chickens we eat are descended from the Red Junglefowl, a member of the pheasant family. Over the centuries they have been bred and fed to produce more flesh and more eggs. In Roman times a chicken laid about 60 eggs a year. By 1925 this number had risen to about 110 in the United States, and today chickens lay as many as 225 per year. Even in poorer, protein starved countries, it is usually easier and cheaper to raise chickens than to go into the forest or onto the plains in search of game birds.

Those who shoot pheasants, grouse and partridges in Europe and North America now rely to some extent on birds raised in pens that are released for the pleasure of the hunters — usually an hour or two before being shot. Pheasants, Gray (or Hungarian) Partridges and Chukars are easily semi-domesticated and can be bred in large numbers. Barring disease, they reproduce well with a high survival rate. One shoot that I know of in Ontario, Canada, raises about 15,000 pheasants each summer.

The order of Galliformes consists of the six principal families mentioned at the beginning of this section, about 269 species in all depending on the authority referred to. The Galliformes range in size from the tiniest quail, which weighs less than two ounces, to the turkey which, in the wild, grows to about 20 pounds. A number of features are common to most of the species. They tend to have full rounded bodies, longish necks, small heads, and short rounded wings. Most species spend much of their feeding time on the ground where their diet consists chiefly of a wide range of vegetable matter, although insects and small vertebrates are taken, particularly during the nesting season.

Seeds are a major source of food. Some soft seeds are eaten, but many are dried and hard, and must be ground to a pulp before entering the intestines. To aid in this process seed-eating birds each day ingest, usually in the afternoon, a quantity of grit in the form of sand or small stones.

Most species nest and roost on the ground, although some fly into trees and bushes at night. Many have wattles and bare patches on the throat and head, most of which are colorful. Colors vary considerably — the females generally being plainer than males. Many species are feathered with rather subdued combinations of brown, black and white. The pheasants, as a group, are the most striking. Some are quite gloriously marked in extravagant patterns of gold, red and blue.

Galliformes are found in most parts of the world and in all kinds of habitat. In North America and Europe the ptarmigans live in fierce Arctic conditions. In Africa and Asia many species live in extreme heat in arid plains. Others live in the rain forests.

The 300 or so species of pigeons have world-wide distribution in more temperate climates. The order has the scientific name of Columbiformes and they are all members of the same family. Pigeons are short-legged, small-headed birds with full bodies. They have relatively soft bills. Seeds and nuts constitute the bulk of their diet.

The sandgrouse group of 16 species is of the order Pteroclidiformes. All belong to the same family. They have rather drab markings of varying shades of brown, with some black and white. Sandgrouse are found in southern Spain, Portugal and France, throughout much of Africa, and in the Middle East, reaching as far as India and China. They are birds of the arid plains.

PHEASANTS AND QUAILS

Crested Francolin (*Francolinus sephaena*)   There are 41 species of francolins widespread in Africa and Asia, of which two reach Europe and the Middle East. Most of these rather similar species have discrete populations in limited areas.

The family Phasianidae, the pheasants and quails, has 183 species of which 21 are considered to be threatened. The family may be divided into four groups: New World quails consisting of 30 species which live from southern Canada to Paraguay; Old World quails, of which there are 11 species, found in Europe, Africa, Asia and Australia; 94 species of partridges found from Europe to Australia; and 48 species of pheasants of which one originates in Africa and the rest in Asia. Several have been introduced to regions outside their place of origin, notably the Ring-necked Pheasant.

A number of features and habits are generally common to the family, although habitat includes such diversity as forests, grasslands, deserts, bushy areas, cultivated land and tundra. Most members of this family are primarily terrestrial, both in feeding and (except for the tragopans) in nesting. They search for their food on the ground, scratching like chickens. They eat seeds, shoots and some insects. Young birds, with an unconscious need for protein, are largely insectivorous. Nesting is almost exclusively on the ground, the nest usually being an indifferently lined scrape in the soil. In some species the sexes are similar in appearance; in others the males are brilliantly colored. Females are generally brown or grey with dark markings. Pheasants and quails tend to have round, squat bodies with short legs; the males have a spur on the tarsus. All are strong runners and seldom fly unless closely attacked or alarmed. In the stubble or under cover they crouch motionless until the last moment when they burst into the air with a flurry of noisy, flapping wings.

The 30 species of New World quails are chunky little birds, usually brown or grey with strong, mostly reddish, markings about the face and neck. Several of the species have flowing head plumes or curly topknots. In North America the best known and most widespread is the Bobwhite Quail. All pair for nesting. After nesting, many join together in coveys of 25 to 30 birds which stay together and exclude newcomers for the rest of the year in a defended territory.

Old World quails are birds of the grasslands of Asia, Australia and Africa. One, the Common Quail, migrates from Africa to Europe and from India to Central Asia during the breeding season. Some other species are nomadic, ranging in flocks to areas where it has rained.

In North America people often refer to most brown, chicken-like, birds as partridges. In fact, the partridge is indigenous only from Europe east to Australia. The Gray (Hungarian) Partridge and the Chukar have been introduced into North America. In Europe and the United Kingdom partridges are in decline. Thirty years ago they were a common sight in fields and meadows but, now, such sightings are rare. The technique of plowing to the fence line leaves nowhere for them to nest, and the intensive use of pesticides has further reduced the stock.

The largest of the partridges is the Tibetan Snowcock found in the mountains of Central Asia. It weighs as much as six and a half pounds. Also included in the group are about 40 species of francolins. Most are indigenous to Africa, but one, the Black Francolin is found in southeastern Europe. It is a splendid bird, mostly black below and reddish on the back.

Pheasants were introduced into Western Europe from the Caucasus and Asia at least 900 years ago. Much later, Far Eastern forms, paler and with a white ring around the neck, were introduced. These interbred with the original stock and with other newcomers, so that there are now many forms. Ring-necked Pheasants nest in forests and hedgerows, but feed in grain fields and pastures during the summer. They were introduced into North America with great success, principally in the prairies of the central United States and southern Canada. They do not do well in the east because of heavier snow cover, for pheasants feed only on the ground. The disinclination to browse in the lower storey of the forest leads to starvation for many birds in heavy snow unless they are fed by humans. In Europe pheasants do better, but in particularly hard winters the wild birds die off in large numbers.

Among the pheasants some of the males may be rated as the most spectacular of birds. The best known in zoos, and as an ornamental bird in large gardens, is the Blue Peacock. The Golden Pheasant of central China, with its absurd gold crest, scarlet belly and 30-inch tail is extraordinary. Over one-third of the world's pheasant species are endangered — partly through killing, but especially as the result of the loss of habitat.

Left: Common Peafowl (*Pavo cristatus*) Although we usually think of "peafowl" as "peacock," the latter name properly applies only to the males. The females (shown here) are known as peahens.

Reeve's Pheasant (*Syrmaticus reevesii*) Of the 48 species of pheasants, all but one originate in Asia. The one, the Congo or African Peacock, was discovered in 1936. Reeve's Pheasant comes from hilly country in central and northern China.

Golden Pheasant (*Chrysolophus pictus*)   By contrast with its gorgeous
mate, the hen is just another chicken-like brown bird with a long
tail. It is native to central China where it is seriously endangered.

Golden Pheasant (*Chrysolophus pictus*) Chinese paintings of the Golden Pheasant arrived in Europe before specimens of the bird itself. There it was dismissed as a gaudy impossibility: people could not believe that such a beautiful bird could exist.

Left: Crimson-bellied Tragopan (*Tragopan temminckii*) The ragged crest, elaborate facial markings and eye ring give this lovely bird a look of mild surprise. Five of the 48 species of pheasant are known as "tragopans."

Lady Amherst Pheasant (*Chrysolophus amherstiae*) Despite its rather delicate and elegant appearance, the Lady Amherst Pheasant is native to high mountains in eastern Tibet and western China. This, and the Golden Pheasant, are also known as Flower pheasants.

Gambel's Quail (*Lophotryx gambelii*) The fine plume on this quail reminds one of the helmet plume of a nineteenth century hussar. It nests on the ground in the dry country of the southwestern United States and northern Mexico.

22

Himalayan Monal Pheasant (*Lophophorus impejanus*)   This female
pheasant is drab in contrast to the colorful male. It is a hardy bird
originating in the Himalayas from Afghanistan, east across Nepal, as
far as northern India.

Elliot's Pheasant (*Syrmaticus ellioti*)   The mountains of Chekiang and Fukien provinces in southeastern China are the only places where this strongly-marked pheasant is found in the wild. Note particularly the white belly and the long barred tail.

Scaled Quail (*Callipepia squamata*)   The population of the Scaled Quail is affected adversely both by drought and by heavy rains. Through much of its range over-grazing has removed brush and bushes which previously provided cover and food.

Right: Silver Pheasant (*Lophura nycthemerus*)   The white tail, finely barred white back, black head and underparts are in striking contrast to the red face and pink legs. The Silver Pheasant lives in mountains from Indochina to China.

Right: Common Peafowl (*Pavo cristatus*) The peafowl prefers to run rather than fly, but will take to the air when flushed, for example, by dogs. Properly launched, it is fast and dextrous in avoidance of tree trunks and other obstacles.

Himalayan Monal Pheasant (*Lophophorus impejanus*) The iridescence, particularly on the gold-and-blue back, is probably the most striking of any bird. Note, too, the contrast with the reddish tail. The topknot is similar to that of some of the quail species of North America.

Common Peafowl (*Pavo cristatus*) Peafowl are native to India and Sri Lanka, but are bred as ornamental birds throughout Europe and America. Their screeches and shrieks cause a disturbance in the early morning.

Right: Montezuma or Harlequin Quail (*Cyrtonyx montezumae*) The elegant and complicated facial pattern gives this bird its alternate name. It also has a brown crest resembling swept-back hair. It lives in high country from Arizona to southern Mexico.

Ring-necked Pheasant (*Phasianus colchicus*)   A dark form of this
species, without a neck ring, was introduced into Europe hundreds
of years ago. It was followed by paler varieties and now all males
have the ring which appears here.

Satyr Tragopan (*Tragopan satyra*) The male shown here displays for its mate by lowering a blue sac from its throat and inflating two blue horns on the crown of its head.

Left: Gambel's Quail (*Lophotryx gambelii*) The Gambel's Quail may be identified by its black face, chestnut crown, black plume and streaked flanks. Not shown here is the black belly patch which usually adorns the male.

California Quail (*Lophotryx californica*) This is a mature female. The male has a black chin and forward leaning topknot. It prefers bushes and rough grass for foraging, and is sometimes seen in residential gardens.

Ring-necked Pheasant (*Phasianus colchicus*)   Pheasants are not
troubled by cold but, since they feed only on the ground, are
doomed in heavy snow unless they are fed. Grouse, in contrast, fly
into trees where they feed on buds and seeds.

Red Junglefowl (*Gallus gallus*) Although the Red Junglefowl is still found in the wild in Asia, its ancestors were domesticated some 5,000 years ago. It is from wild stock of this bird that domestic poultry is descended. It is still used for cockfighting in some places.

Chukar (*Alectoris chukar*) The Chukar or Chukar Partridge is native to Greece, through eastern Europe and the Middle East as far as Pakistan. In Europe it has become scarce due to intensive use of pesticides. Its name comes from its call "chuk, chuk, chuk, chukar."

Pallas' Snow or Blue-eared Pheasant (*Crossoptilon auritum*) This handsome blue pheasant with a long bushy tail and red legs is a native of the mountainous country in the northwest corner of China, and from there into Mongolia.

Red-billed Francolin (*Francolinus adspersus*) The Red-billed Francolin is grey and evenly colored. Most francolins are predominantly brown and many are heavily speckled. The bright red bill on this bird is unusual.

Left: Bobwhite (*Colinus virginianus*) The Bobwhite receives its name from its call which rises somewhat on the second syllable. It is widespread in brush country throughout the United States and south to Guatemala.

Bobwhite (*Colinus virginianus*) During the non-breeding season, Bobwhite congregate in coveys of about 30 birds. The covey defends its territory against intruders. The Bobwhite is heavily hunted in the United States.

Swainson's Spurfowl (*Pternistis swainsonii*) There are four members of the spurfowl group, closely related to the partridges. All are members of the Phasianidae family. This one lives only in Zimbabwe.

Korean Ring-necked Pheasant
(*Phasianus colchicus karpowi*)
The Korean Ring-necked
Pheasant is similar to but larger
than the Chinese Ring-necked
Pheasant. The mantle and
flanks are a dark golden yellow
and the crown is a light
grey-green.

Yellow-necked Spurfowl
(*Pternistis leucoscepus*)   The four
spurfowl species are more erect
in posture than other
partridges. Their height is
made more apparent by their
long legs. They live in brush
country, feeding principally on
seeds and some insects.

Left: Chukar (*Alectoris chukar*) The Chukar is very similar to the Rock Partridge, but their ranges overlap only in Greece. It has been introduced as a captive bird for shooting in Europe and North America where it is quite easy to breed.

Barbary Partridge (*Alectoris barbara*) The Barbary Partridge is a species of rock partridge. It has brown and grey plumage barred with black, brown and white at the sides of the body, while the beak, eyecombs and legs are bright red.

Crested Green
Wood Partridge
(*Rollulus roulroul*)
The dark blue back,
red face and reddish
crest combine to
give this splendid
bird a truly exotic
appearance. It lives
in the forests of
Malaysia and
Thailand.

Yellow-necked Spurfowl (*Pternistis leucoscepus*) This spurfowl is resident from Somalia southward through Ethiopia, Kenya and Uganda to Tanzania.

47

Lady Amherst Pheasant (*Chrysolophus amherstiae*)   The dramatic white, green and black body feathers of the Lady Amherst Pheasant vie for attention with the striking spiky red feathers under the tail. Like most pheasants, it adapts well to captivity and breeds successfully.

Right: Satyr Tragopan (*Tragopan satyra*)   Although this bird is a pheasant, the facial markings remind one of a quail. This one is native to Nepal and to neighboring Sikkim and Bhutan, all of which border northern India.

GROUSE

Left: Barbary Partridge (*Alectoris barbara*)   There are 94 species of partridge. The Barbary lives across North Africa, in Sardinia and in Gibraltar. Its habitat varies from desert, stony plains and hillsides to open woodland.

Sharp-tailed Grouse (*Pedioecetes phasianellus*)   The range extends from northern Alaska, across northern Canada to western Quebec, and south to Oregon and east to Michigan. Although not strictly migratory, it becomes nomadic in particularly hard winters.

Grouse are chicken-like birds of the Northern Hemisphere — not unlike pheasants and partridges. There are 16 species of which one, the Rock Ptarmigan, occurs across the northern part of North America and Eurasia, and the rest only in North America or Eurasia. One species, the Willow Ptarmigan of North America is almost (except for molting patterns) indistinguishable from the Willow Grouse of the Eastern Hemisphere. Few people in settled parts have ever seen ptarmigan which are found only in the high mountains in the north, but they are well known from photographs because many molt to pure white plumage in winter.

Grouse have short rounded wings, powered by robust muscles. Most North Americans who have spent time in the northern woods have been alarmed by a Ruffed Grouse bursting from cover at their feet. The whirring and flurried takeoff is typical of the grouse family. They fly for a short distance and then go into a long glide, usually followed by another series of flaps. The far northern species are hardy and can survive low temperatures and heavy snow by feeding on buds, needles and other fibrous material of low nutrient value. They have large crops and gizzards for storing and digesting this monotonous winter diet, but they must ingest grit regularly to aid the process. At the end of the day, northern grouse may dive into the soft snow for protection from the wind and for the relative warmth it provides during the night. Many birds die if there is a thaw followed by nighttime freezing which may form an entrapping crust of ice.

In summer the diet becomes more varied and includes shoots, fresh buds and insects.

Some species of grouse lead solitary lives, pairing only during the nesting season. Others, including Sharp-tailed Grouse, prairie chickens and Sage Grouse of the North American prairies, and the curly-tailed Black Grouse of Europe, come together during the breeding season on stamping areas known as "leks." The same patch of ground may be used year after year. Here the males congregate, inflate their colorful air sacs, display by fanning their tails and make loud booming noises. Females are attracted to the lek and choose a mate. The female then scrapes a nest in the ground, and incubates her large clutch alone. Grouse chicks run about shortly after hatching and, for the most part, find their own food.

In North America large numbers of grouse are shot, particularly the Ruffed Grouse in the northern forests and the Sharp-tailed and Sage grouse in the prairies. The Greater and Lesser prairie chickens have limited ranges. They are now uncommon and in decline. The Atwater's Prairie Chicken, a smaller, dark form of the Greater Prairie Chicken, is seriously endangered, now restricted to a small area of southern Texas.

In Europe the Willow Grouse (or Ptarmigan) and the attractively marked Hazelhen (or Hazel Grouse) have the widest distribution. In the British Isles the Willow Grouse is replaced by a separate race of the same species known as the Red Grouse, or just plain Grouse. This race does not molt to white in winter as does the Scandinavian race. The British race is restricted to the moors of the British Isles where it is a favored game bird. In Scotland, shooting traditionally begins on the twelfth of August, a date known to shooting people as "the Glorious Twelfth."

The largest grouse is the Capercaillie which lives in northern Scotland and in mountainous country in Europe. The male is a three-foot-long, 14-pound bird, which habitually feeds and roosts in coniferous trees. Like the prairie chickens, it forms leks during the breeding season where it displays and pours forth a remarkable song of raucous squawks and gurgles, like liquid pouring from a bottle.

Left: Ruffed Grouse (*Bonasa umbellus*)   The most widespread and abundant of all North American grouse, it lives in wooded areas from Alaska south throughout much of the continent north of Mexico. It is non-migratory, and a family or small group can sustain itself in small patches of forest.

Blue Grouse (*Dendragapus obscurus*)   This large grouse is nearly two feet long. In winter it lives mainly in conifers, feeding on the needles. Its range extends from southern Alaska to the mountains of Arizona and California.

Spruce Grouse (*Canachites canadensis*)   The male puffs itself up in an extraordinary mating display. The red skin over the eyes is hugely inflated. It is so unafraid of humans that it can easily be killed with a stick, and has accordingly earned the name "fool hen."

Right: Sage Grouse (*Centrocerus urophasianus*)   This photograph shows the remarkable tapered tail feathers of the displaying male. This posturing is used to establish territory and to attract females.

Left: Rock Ptarmigan (*Lagopus mutus*)   The Rock Ptarmigan lives in mountainous areas. This photograph shows Mount McKinley, Alaska, in the background.

White-tailed Ptarmigan (*Lagopus leucurus*)   Shown here in summer plumage, the legs of this ptarmigan are feathered to the toes. Resident on both sides of the Rocky Mountains from Alaska south to the northern United States, some birds have been introduced into several other states.

Left: Willow Ptarmigan or Willow Grouse (*Lagopus lagopus*) The hen lays her eggs in a variety of protected locations. This chick may have hatched at the edge of a coastal beach or at any altitude up to high moors, including treeless tundra.

Sharp-tailed Grouse (*Pedioecetes phasianellus*) This is the common grouse of the prairies, usually incorrectly called "prairie chicken," which is a totally different species. It prefers to feed in the open, usually in clearings in coniferous areas.

Left: Lesser Prairie Chicken (*Tympanuchus pallidicinctus*)   Slightly smaller and more finely barred than the Greater Prairie Chicken, the Lesser is now restricted to the grasslands in parts of Colorado, Kansas, Oklahoma and Texas.

Greater Prairie Chicken or Pinnated Grouse (*Tympanuchus cupido*)   This species was once common, and was resident through the prairies of North America. The population has declined seriously due to habitat destruction and shooting. The remaining birds live in isolated patches in the central United States.

Left: Rock Ptarmigan (*Lagopus mutus*)   In Europe and Asia this bird lives in the extreme north, in the Alps and in the Pyrenees. It is also widely distributed in northern North America. Its winter plumage is pure white.

White-tailed Ptarmigan (*Lagopus leucurus*)   During the winter this species descends from the rocky, alpine meadows into the protection of the timber. Other ptarmigan have black tail feathers, but this one is all white: it is marvellously camouflaged against the snow.

Right: Sage Grouse (*Centrocerus urophasianus*) The sage bush is vital to the survival of the Sage Grouse for its seeds constitute about three-quarters of the mature bird's summer diet. In winter it seldom eats anything else. Young birds feed on ants, grasshoppers and other insects.

Sharp-tailed Grouse (*Pedioecetes phasianellus*) Here the grouse is displaying on the lekking ground. Note the inflated orange-yellow comb and the bare violet area on the neck. The long central tail feathers give the bird its name.

Left: Rock Ptarmigan (*Lagopus mutus*)   In summer, the Rock Ptarmigan molts the white feathers on back and sides and grows brown ones. These feathers turn to grey in autumn and pure white in winter.

Lesser Prairie Chicken (*Tympanuchus pallidicinctus*)   The pouch on either side of the neck is inflated during the ritual mating display. The pouch on the Lesser is smaller and darker than that on the Greater Prairie Chicken. The bowing posture is common to several grouse species.

White-tailed Ptarmigan (*Lagopus leucurus*) Unlike most grouse, the male of this species appears to be monogamous and remains with the hen until the eggs hatch. The young feed themselves, and can fly short distances when they are 10 to 20 days old.

Right: Willow Ptarmigan (*Lagopus lagopus*) Ptarmigan are both ground and tree feeders. Appropriately, the most important winter food for this species in North America consists of the buds and twigs of willows.

Preceding pages: Sage Grouse (*Centrocerus urophasianus*) The Sage Grouse was once far more abundant than today. Closed seasons in several western states and in Canada during the 1950s have led to some recovery. Shooting now accounts for about 250,000 birds each year.

Spruce Grouse (*Canachites canadensis*) In summer this grouse eats ground vegetation such as blueberry leaves and berries. During the autumn it increases its intake of conifer needles which constitute its entire diet in winter.

Ruffed Grouse
(*Bonasa umbellus*)
In the autumn the
Ruffed Grouse is
one of the most
sought after game
birds. It is found
singly or in groups
of two or three as it
explodes into short
flights.

Left: Willow Ptarmigan (*Lagopus lagopus*) In Europe this species is known as the Willow Grouse. The race resident in the British isles is very dark and does not grow white feathers in winter. There it is known as Red Grouse, or just plain Grouse.

Willow Ptarmigan or Willow Grouse (*Lagopus lagopus*) In winter the Willow can be distinguished from the Rock Ptarmigan only by the absence of a black line on the face of the male. The Rock Ptarmigan is circumpolar at high latitudes.

Left: Greater Prairie Chicken or Pinnated Grouse (*Tympanuchus cupido*)   On the lekking ground where grouse meet to display and mate, the males adopt a variety of postures, make booming calls and cackles. This one is "flutter-jumping," a form of display most often undertaken by peripheral males — those not yet able to dominate the lek.

Greater Prairie Chicken (*Tympanuchus cupido*)   All species of prairie chicken are now to some extent endangered, as a result both of destruction of habitat and shooting.

Right: Blue Grouse (*Dendragapus obscurus*) This is a female with fairly well developed young in mid-summer. The female usually lays between seven and 10 eggs, but it is unusual for the full clutch to mature.

Spruce Grouse (*Canachites canadensis*) A forest species, the Spruce Grouse lives north to the tree line across Canada and in a few of the northern States. It lives almost entirely in coniferous forests.

Ruffed Grouse (*Bonasa umbellus*)   As part of its courtship ritual, the grouse beats its wings in a flurry gradually decreasing in speed and force. In spring this "drumming" can be heard for some distance.

TURKEYS

Ocellated Turkey (*Agriocharis ocellata*)   This turkey is much smaller than the Common Turkey. It is resident from southern Mexico to Guatemala and Belize.

When the Spaniards arrived in Mexico early in the sixteenth century, the Common Turkey ranged from what is now the northern United States south to Guatemala, wherever the forest was suitable. It is believed that turkeys were domesticated long before this in Mexico. The smaller Ocellated Turkey lives from the Yucatan Peninsula south to Guatemala. During the nineteenth century turkeys were so common in the United States that large flocks did considerable damage in grain fields. Originally turkeys were not particularly shy, but with the introduction of guns they became extremely wary.

Heavy shooting, and the disappearance of the forests where they feed and roost, reduced to remnants both the range and number of turkeys. They prefer somewhat open woods with frequent clearings. Here they feed principally on acorns; the disappearance of the chestnut, due to the chestnut blight, eliminated what was probably their main food previously. During the last few decades wild birds have been reintroduced into forests where they once lived, and the stock is improving. They only succeed in extensive tracts. They require one square mile for every two to five birds, although, where food is plentiful, a larger population can maintain itself. Selective logging often improves the habitat for turkeys, for the opening of the forest canopy creates clearings where new cover grows, and where smaller trees remain to provide food. They eat the seeds of many kinds of trees and plants, as well as insects, salamanders and snakes. In the forest they compete for food with deer and ranging pigs, but often lose out.

Although they are strong fliers, turkeys seldom take to the air unless alarmed, or when flying into the branches of a tree to roost. For the night they seem to prefer the upper branches of pines and firs. From a perch they take off in a long glide which, if starting from high ground, may be as long as a mile.

The mating and breeding patterns of turkeys are highly structured. A dominant male may establish a group of several females and, in maintaining the group, will have to defend it, and his territory, against the challenge of younger and less experienced males. The male is equipped with spurs. Fights may last for as long as an hour or two, and may result in the death of a challenger or the challenged. When they have mated, the females go off alone to lay and incubate their large clutch of eight to 15 eggs in a scrape on the ground. The young are out of the nest within a day of hatching, and fly well enough to roost and fend for themselves after four weeks. After about six months young males form close groups which stay together. Young females remain in family groups forming flocks.

The male turkey is a dark, bronzed bird with iridescent feathers on the back, breast and wings. The head is unfeathered, red in the Common Turkey and blue in the Ocellated. Males may weigh as much as 20 pounds. Domesticated birds may reach 40 pounds. The tips of the tail feathers and upper wing coverts vary from brown to white, the Mexican race being white. The male has a long tuft hanging from its breast and inflatable wattles on the throat. On mating the male puffs up its body feathers and wattles and fans its tail upward in an elaborate display of strutting and stamping.

Common Turkey
(*Meleagris gallopavo*)
During the breeding
season the male
develops a thick sac
on the chest in
which is stored
fat.

Common Turkey (*Meleagris gallopavo*) In the wild turkeys grow to as much as 20 pounds. Some domesticated birds may weigh twice that. Females are about half the weight of the male.

Common Turkey (*Meleagris gallopavo*) Turkeys are polygamous in that a dominant male may mate with several females. Young males must wait several years to dominate a patriarch.

GUINEA FOWL

Left: Common Turkey (*Meleagris gallopavo*)   In pre-colonial times the Common Turkey was abundant from southern Canada to Guatemala. As recently as the nineteenth century it was considered a pest by farmers, but is now rare and found only in large forests.

Helmeted Guinea Fowl (*Numida mitrata*)   Flocks of up to 2,000 birds may gather during the dry season where they remain in a limited area close to a source of water. They also require trees or bushes in which to roost.

The six species of guinea fowl are found naturally only in Africa. They derive the name from the part of the continent — Guinea — from which the world-wide domesticated stock originated. They are smaller than most chickens and most have dark, spotted and lined plumage. All have almost bare heads adorned with either a bony casque or a tuft of feathers. The skin on the head varies from cobalt blue to dark red.

Guinea fowl feed on the ground on seeds, tubers, roots and grain for most of the year, but during the wet season they turn increasingly to insects. At night they roost in bushes or, for preference, in trees. During the non-breeding season they form flocks varying from 10 to 40 birds for most species. The Helmeted Guinea Fowl, however, will congregate in groups of as many as 2,000 birds in the dry season. This occurs in areas where water and food is patchy and where such a flock may find abundant food in a restricted locality. Here the flock may remain for months, wandering only a mile or two from the source of water.

At the approach of the nesting season the urge to mate prompts the males to assert themselves over other males. They engage in highly ritualized mock battles in which they chase one another, with wings raised while held close to the body, and with the head lowered. Up to eight or 10 birds may be involved, each chasing the other in single file. Females seem to be attracted by this display and pairs are formed. In the wild it is seldom that these battles develop into a genuine attack, but in captivity, where there is no escape, fights to the death sometimes occur. The pair bonds that are formed during courtship are temporary, lasting, in the first instance, until incubation begins in a nest scraped in the ground. The male then wanders away for a few days but returns before the young are hatched. When this happens the chicks, or "keets," are away from the nest and foraging for themselves after one or two days. They are particularly vulnerable in the two weeks before they can fly, and the male is attentive during this period. Flocks break up during nesting, but re-form to include the young birds which are gathered together in the center of the flock. This provides protection of a sort against predators like jackals and snakes.

The habitat used by this family of birds varies considerably. The White-breasted and Black guinea fowl prefer rain forests, leaving for drier ground during the wettest part of the year. The rest inhabit territory varying from dry scrub and open dry forest to desert. The Vulturine Guinea Fowl appears to be able to survive in country where there is virtually no water.

It is the Helmeted Guinea Fowl that is best known as a domesticated bird — indeed it is found on farms and dinner tables all over the world. In the wild this species is in trouble. It was formerly common north of the Sahara in Morocco, but is now probably extinct there, due to habitat destruction and shooting.

In West Africa the White-breasted Guinea Fowl is heavily threatened due to the destruction of its habitat, the rain forests.

Left: Helmeted Guinea Fowl (*Numida mitrata*) There are eight species of guinea fowl, all resident only in Africa. The Helmeted Guinea Fowl is widespread from Uganda to South Africa.

Helmeted Guinea Fowl (*Numida Mitrata*) The casque or helmet is actually a bony structure. In this species the wattles on the throat may be bright blue (as here) or red. The sexes are similar in appearance, but their calls differ.

Vulturine Guinea Fowl (*Acryllium vulturinum*) This is the largest member of the guinea fowl family. It has a band of short brown feathers across the back of the head and a hackle of long loose feathers covering the breast and back.

Tufted Guinea Fowl (*Numida meleagris*)   Note the tiny head and the
way it relates to the full, rounded body. This species lives from
Sudan south through Ethiopia and Uganda to Kenya.

MEGAPODES

Brush Turkey (*Alectura lathami*)   The Brush Turkey is not a turkey, although it resembles one. It is a member of the Megapode family of mound builders. It lives in the moist forests of eastern Australia. It seldom flies, preferring to run or walk.

The 16 species of this strange family of Galliformes are most unlikely game birds. They are indifferent fliers, mostly large and ungainly, preferring always to walk and to hide. They are usually described as "mound birds" which indicates the habit of all species of building mounds, some huge, of earth, sand and vegetation in which they lay their eggs. Three species, the Mallee Fowl, Brush Turkey and Scrub Fowl, live in Australia; the rest live in the islands to the north, in the Philippines, New Guinea, Malaysia and other islands.

The habit of burying their eggs, common to all the megapodes, sets this family apart from other birds. The technique of mound building varies considerably between species, but what is common to all is the care that the parents, most often the male, take in regulating the temperature. The bird tests the heat regularly by prodding its head deep into the mound covering. A sensitive gland on the bill tests the temperature, which is then adjusted by removing or adding cover. Heat comes from the sun, from rotting leaf litter or, in the case of the Common Scrub Fowl in the Solomon Islands, from hot underground volcanic streams and gases. The preferred temperature is from 90 to 93 degrees Fahrenheit.

When the first explorers arrived in Australia and saw the mounds made by the megapodes, they thought that they were the burial mounds of the Aborigines. They must have seen the nests of the Common Scrub Fowl which are enormous, some as much as 36 feet in diameter and as high as 16 feet. One mound may be in use for centuries and be used by several pairs of the same species or even pairs of different species. Others are more modest, some 10 to 15 feet across and four feet high. Some mounds have been in use for so long that they are examined by archaeologists to determine the historical occurrence of fire and drought.

Mounds are worked spasmodically by male and female birds throughout the year. During the non-breeding season they add earth and litter. On mounds that are shared by a number of pairs, each pair works in turn.

The Maleo Fowl of the Celebes Islands do not build mounds. They walk long distances, often about 20 miles from the rain forest to the sandy beaches, where the male digs a number of holes. The female deposits a single egg into each hole which is then warmed by the sun and by decomposing litter.

Eggs are laid, for most species, several days apart, between September and January. The male then covers the excavation for the fresh egg with leaves and soil. The number of eggs laid by each female during the breeding season varies considerably between species and between pairs of the same species. Observed clutches have ranged from as few as five eggs to as many as 31. Most bird species lay their eggs a day or so apart, and begin incubation only when the clutch is complete. Not the megapodes. With them, incubation starts immediately and the young are hatched in series after 50 to 90 days. They may never see their parents, for, upon hatching, they scratch their way upward and are able to fend for themselves from the start. Within a week they are capable of flight. In the case of the Maleo Fowl in the Celebes, the hatchlings are capable of walking the 10 to 20 miles to the jungle where they live.

Although megapodes are capable of short flights, they seldom take to the air. To roost in trees at night several of the forest species walk up an inclined or broken trunk to roost. On such trees, the bark may be worn away on the upper surface by the claws of the climbers.

In Australia the three resident species live in separate parts of the country. The Mallee Fowl lives across the southern half of the country, except in the extreme east, in the dry brush or "mallee" scrub of the dry plains. The Australian Brush Turkey inhabits the moist forests of the eastern coastal region where its numbers are in serious decline, primarily due to the elimination of the forests. The Scrub Fowl, a dark brown bird with a pronounced crest, lives across the tropical rain forests of the north.

Most of the species are subject to heavy predation from humans who kill them for food, and take eggs in large numbers. On some islands egg taking is carefully controlled. Large lizards and monitors also take eggs, as do introduced foxes.

Mallee Fowl (*Leipoa ocellata*)
Mallee Fowl hens lay eggs
periodically in their mounds
between September and
January, usually about 20 in all.
The eggs hatch in 50 to 90
days and the young fend for
themselves from the start.

Mallee Fowl (*Leipoa ocellata*)
The 16 species of mound-
building birds live on islands
of the western Pacific and
eastern Indian oceans, and in
Australia. The Mallee Fowl
lives in dry areas of mallee
scrub in southern Australia.

Mallee Fowl Mound.   The mound birds in Australia deposit their eggs in a pile of sand and grass which they build, and cover them with sand. Egg temperature is regulated by adding or removing part of the cover. The mound shown here is 15 feet in diameter and about three feet high.

Brush Turkey (*Alectura lathami*)   The wattle of the male is inflated
during courtship. Megapodes tend the nest mound, regulating the
temperature while the eggs are incubating, but the newly hatched
chick scratches its own way to the surface.

CHACHALACAS, GUANS, CURASSOWS

Rufous-vented Chachalaca (*Ortalis ruficauda*)   This dark brown species of chachalaca has a bare red throat patch and a long wide tail. It scratches the litter on the forest floor with its strong claws for most of its food.

The family of birds known by their scientific name of Cracidae live from the extreme southern part of Texas, through Central America, and in the warmer parts of South America. The 44 species are large game birds, much more arboreal than other groups. Guans feed and nest in trees and scrub, but the curassows and chachalacas spend much of their time on the ground and may nest there.

Throughout their range the Cracidae are much favored as food by local people. Increasing hunting pressure and habitat destruction have reduced some species to remnant groups of only a few birds. Most species live in the forests which are disappearing around them. As an example, the White-winged Guan which was thought to have become extinct more than 100 years ago, was rediscovered in 1977. The few remaining birds were in a forest which has since been cut. The members of the family are poor fliers and, although they become shy under shooting pressure, are slow flying, easy targets. Many are shot while perched in trees.

As a group the chachalacas, guans and curassows range in size from a turkey to a mid-sized chicken. They have blunt wings, long wide tails, long legs, full bodies and small heads. They are a noisy group, travelling about in flocks of up to 100 birds, calling with chortles, booms and extraordinary whistles, making an otherwise quiet forest ring with sound. They are noisiest in the early morning and the evening. It has been suggested that some of the members of this group have the most resounding call of all birds.

Of the three groups of the family Cracidae, the chachalacas are usually the easiest to find, for they appear to be comfortable near people. They usually feed in scrub quite close to the ground. One will see, first, a large brown form flying a short distance and disappearing into the undergrowth, then another and another, the forest swallowing each in succession. Chachalacas get their name from their raucous calls which can be startling, "cha-cha-la-ca."

The 19 species of guans are larger than the chachalacas. The largest, the Crested Guan, is 36 inches long. Nearly half its length is tail. As a group, guans are more colorful than chachalacas. Several possess dark green backs with a glossy sheen. Many have long head feathers showing as crests.

The largest birds in the family are among the curassows. They are weak fliers and spend their time close to the ground. Curassows display a remarkable collection of facial adornments, wattles, and, on the head, curly crests. Two species, the Horned and Helmeted curassows, have bony horns protruding from the head.

Wattled Curassow (*Crax globulosa*) The wattles of the male at the base of the bill may be either red or yellow. The Wattled Curassow lives in the forests of the Amazon basin from Equador south to northern Bolivia.

103

Left: Great Curassow (*Crax rubra*) This very large member of the Cracidae family may be more than three feet long. It is handsome, with its curly feathered crest and yellow knob at the base of the upper bill. It is now rare, found only in remote forests.

Rufous-vented Chachalaca (*Ortalis ruficauda*) This is a South American species which is found only in Colombia, Venezuela and in the West Indies. Although it is a ground feeder, it flies into trees when threatened. The nest may be on the ground or in low branches.

Plain Chachalaca (*Ortalis vetula*)   Slow flyers and good to eat, chachalacas are mercilessly hunted in Central and South America. They belong to the family of guans and curassows, all threatened by destruction of forests.

Plain Chachalaca (*Ortalis vetula*)   The raucous call of the Chachalaca closely resembles the sound of its name. It feeds on fruit, leaves, buds and the occasional insect, mainly on, or close to the ground in low bushes and in the forest.

PIGEONS

Left: White-bellied Chachalaca (*Ortalis leucogastra*)   The chachalacas are large birds, up to 30 inches long, and quite similar to one another. This one lives on the Pacific slope from Chiapas in southern Mexico to northern Nicaragua. The tail has a pure white tip.

Ring-necked Dove (*Streptopelia capicola*)   The distinct black band at the nape of the neck is a clearly distinguishing feature of this African species. It is widespread and quite common from the Sudan and Ethiopia to South Africa.

Pigeons and doves belong to the order of birds known as Columbiformes, and all the 300 or so species are members of the same family, Columbidae. They are found in all parts of the world, from the Arctic Circle south to the end of the land, but not including Antarctica or the far north. They are great colonizers, having spread to most remote islands. Curiously, they failed to reach the Hawaiian group, but some species have been introduced there. Of the 300 species of pigeons and doves, approximately one-half may reasonably be said to inhabit a restricted area, either a single island or group of adjacent islands, or a small part of a continent. It is likely that early colonizers of such areas were members of different species which, over time, have become differentiated sufficiently to become separate species. The greatest concentrations of such groups are in the islands between Australia and Asia where rich flora exist, and where sea distances between islands are great.

The members of many families of birds differ so much one from another, that appearance alone may make it impossible to determine a relationship. As an example, the pheasant family includes such unlikely cousins as the Blue Peacock and the tiny Bobwhite Quail with few common physical features. Pigeons and doves, however, look like pigeons and doves. They are stocky, full-bodied birds with small heads, short bills and short legs. They tend to have muted, unspectacular coloring in combinations of pale browns, grey, blue and pink. The males and females of almost all the species are similar, but the female may be somewhat paler. Most have longish tails — some narrow, and some fanned. The Mourning Dove of North America can be distinguished instantly when perched on wires or in the air by its long narrow tail.

Most species of pigeons nest in trees in nests made of twigs. Others, like the Rock Dove, prefer crevices, and have adapted to using overhangs in buildings, barns and the undersides of bridges. Still others use natural cavities in cliffs, holes in trees or burrows in the soil.

All fly strongly. Many make migratory flights of thousands of miles. The flight muscles are so well developed that they make up about one-third of the weight of the bird. They are noisy when they take off, for the wings then flap together. It is thought that this may constitute an alarm signal, putting the rest of the flock to flight. On landing, pigeons cruise downward with the wings held high in a narrow "V."

The vocal range of this family of birds is limited. Most species call with variations of cooing, some monotonous and mournful, others a single gentle note. In the forests a birder may spend several minutes searching high in the distant trees to locate a sound, only to find that the bird is only a few feet away — such is the ventriloqual quality of the cooing.

An unusual habit among pigeons occurs when they drink. Most birds take in a small quantity of water and then raise their heads to swallow.

Pigeons, however, immerse their bills to the nostrils and suck water in until they are finished.

Despite the similarity of shape, pigeons range considerably in size from less than six inches to some 33 inches in length, and in weight from one ounce to over five pounds.

Pigeons eat a wide range of vegetable matter, including green leaves and shoots, seeds, grain and, in tropical countries, soft fruit. In large numbers they can become serious pests in some farming areas. The seed-eating species have strong gizzards adapted to grinding hard matter with grit that is regularly ingested. The fruit-eating species feed in the forest trees of the tropics which, in season, produce a multitude of small berries and fruits. These are swallowed whole. The digestive system uses only the pulp, the seeds being voided. In this way, pigeons form an important part of the eco-logical whole, for they disperse seeds over a wide area, some to germinate, others to provide food for various forms of insect and animal life.

All pigeons almost always lay one or two eggs per clutch. Like other birds, they produce a clutch of a size that creates the best conditions for the survival of the young. Pigeons probably can't feed more than one or two at a time. Because pheasants' young can feed themselves right away, more can be raised in a single brood. The incubation period for pigeons is short and the young are fledged quickly. The female often lays the ensuing clutch before the young bird, or birds, have left the nest. In some warm parts of the world, where the parents do not have to migrate, as many as eight clutches may be raised in succession.

An unusual feature among pigeons is the production by both parents of "pigeon milk." This is a high-protein substance possessing characteristics similar to the milk produced by mammals. It is formed in the crop and fed directly to the young birds. For the first few days after hatching this is the only food the young receive. Later on it is mixed in the crop with vegetable matter and some insects. This weaning process continues until the young leave the nest.

The pigeon that most people who live in cities or agricultural areas know is the Rock Dove or feral pigeon, which has a worldwide distribution. In the pure form it has a purplish front and neck, grey wings, back and tail, with a black tip. For centuries this bird has been domesticated, or semi-domesticated, and has hybridized with other species. As a result we now see a strange mixture of coloring in birds in urban parks, from the pure form, to birds mottled with pale brown, patches of white to pure white. It is this bird that makes up the stock of "racing" pigeons, or "homing" pigeons, birds used in a pastime more popular in Europe than it is in North America. These birds are taken for long distances and, on release, return to their natal dovecote, some at an average speed of about 45 miles per hour.

Many species of pigeons, such as the Mourning Dove of North America, have benefitted from the spread of humans due to a reduction in the numbers of predators, and an increase in their food supply from the forest and from hand-outs, and an increase in the number of suitable nesting sites. Other forest-dwelling species have not fared well, and several are pressed to survive due to a constant destruction of habitat.

The most dramatic example of the reduction to final extinction of a bird species is the story of the Passenger Pigeon. During the early part of the nineteenth century, and earlier, it was probably the most numerous bird species in North America. Some authorities have estimated, or guessed, that the population exceeded three billion birds. The birds moved about the forested areas of eastern North America in immense flocks from one feeding area to another. They would settle in trees, taking acorns, chestnuts and other nuts and fruit, and remain until the food was gone. Nests crowded the trees, sometimes up to 100 per tree. John James Audubon, the great artist and naturalist, has left a description of one migrating flock that he saw in Kentucky in 1813. He said that "the light of the noon day sun was obscured as by an eclipse." He estimated that the flock was one mile wide and that, passing at 60 miles per hour, would, in three hours, account for 1,115,136,000 birds. He reckoned that "the quantity [of food] necessary for supplying this vast multitude must be 8,712,000 bushels per day."

Two things happened. First, huge numbers were killed for food — they were either shot or clubbed as they roosted at night. Train loads of dead birds were shipped to the cities as human food, and hogs were driven, often for long distances, to fatten on the carcasses on the ground. Second, it was impossible for these multitudes to survive in the face of expanding agriculture, and the cutting of the forests.

It is not known what finally caused extinction but, by 1870, the only flocks left were in the forests near the Great Lakes. It seems certain that when the great forests and huge flocks were destroyed, the female would no longer nest or breed. The last free bird was shot in 1899, and the last bird in the world died in the Cincinnati zoo in September 1, 1914.

In some areas flocks of pigeons move into fields of grain and do heavy damage. In the cities the feral pigeons not only deface buildings, but their droppings also constitute a minor health hazard.

Some species are spreading. The attractive Collared Dove started spreading northward through Europe in about 1900. It first nested in the United Kingdom in 1930 where it is now common. In some parts of Europe and England the Wood Pigeon is a much sought "sporting" bird. During the nesting season it is quite tame, but when one is carrying a gun it becomes wary.

Rock Dove or Feral Pigeon (*Columba livia*)   This bird's ancestors were wild birds from Europe, Asia and Africa, which nested on cliffs near the sea. Centuries of domestication and mixed breeding have produced the varieties of coloration now to be seen.

Band-tailed Pigeon (*Columba fasciata*)   This is a forest pigeon
distributed from the western United States to northern Argentina. It
nests up to 10,000 feet and descends to the lowlands when not
breeding. Numbers are much reduced due to shooting and forest
destruction.

Galapagos Dove (*Nesopelia galapagoensis*)   Generally, the bird species
resident on the Galapagos Islands started as "accidentals" and
gradually became specific species. Most, like these doves, are dull
brown in color, and are very tame.

Left: Inca Dove (*Scardafella inca*) The belly and chest have a scalloped appearance. In the United States it is sometimes found as far north as Kansas and Oklahoma.

Inca Dove (*Scardafella inca*) The Inca Dove is slender and grey with a rather long, square-ended tail. It is common in scrub and around towns and farms from the southwestern United States to Costa Rica.

Namaqua Dove (*Oena capensis*)   A very small dove, with a long tail
and a black patch on the throat, the Namaqua is resident from Israel
south through the Arabian Peninsula, from Sudan eastward in
Africa, and in Madagascar.

White-fronted or White-tipped Dove (*Leptotila verreauxi*) This dove is common from southern Texas to Argentina. Although timid, it often feeds on lawns in residential areas, but is usually found in second growth woodland. It ranges from sea level to 6,000 feet.

Left: White-winged Dove (*Zenaida asiatica*) During the breeding season the White-winged Dove moves to dry scrubby areas in much of its range. It resembles the Mourning Dove quite closely, but for the white wing patches.

Mourning Dove (*Zenaidura macroura*) The plain coral color and white edges on the long wedged tail easily identify this bird. It is seen from roads on power lines and fence wires.

Ringed Turtle Dove (*Streptopelia risoria*) Pigeons and doves are unusual in that they produce "milk" in their crops which the young reach with their bills. The milk is quite similar to that produced by mammals.

Ringed Turtle Dove (*Streptopelia risoria*) With a widespread distribution throughout much of the world, turtle doves are strong fliers. They migrate thousands of miles — usually in easy stages. Wing muscles make up nearly one-third of their weight.

Victoria Crowned Pigeon (*Goura victoria*) This is the glamor bird of all the pigeons and also the largest. The exotic crown of white-tipped blue feathers and the blue body are quite extraordinary.

Left: White-winged Dove (*Zenaida asiatica*) The white wing patch identifies this dove both when perched or in flight. It lives from the southwestern United States south to Costa Rica and occasionally Panama, Equador, Chile and in the Bahamas and Antilles.

Spotted Dove (*Streptopelia chinensis*) Native to India and parts of China, the Spotted Dove has been introduced into the United States, Mauritius, Hawaii and into several of the Indonesian Islands where it thrives.

Left: Mourning Dove (*Zenaidura macroura*)   This slender, long-tailed dove is found from southern Alaska south to Panama. It is common throughout eastern North America and in some parts of the West Indies. Some wintering birds now remain as far north as Ontario.

Speckled Pigeon (*Columba guinea*)   The Speckled Pigeon is quite large and handsomely marked with large white spots on the wings and back. It is a resident African bird which lives from Ethiopia in the north to South Africa.

Common Ground Dove (*Columbina passerina*)   There are 10 species
of ground doves resident in North and South America. All are small
in relation to other doves, and feed almost entirely on the ground.
The Common Ground Dove is widespread from the southern United
States to northern South America.

WOODCOCK AND SNIPE

Common Snipe (*Capella gallinago*) Snipe and woodcock are members of the family of sandpipers. They are shot for sport and food.

The four families in the order Charadiiformes, all generally known as "waders" or "wading birds," are the plovers, sandpipers, avocets and stilts, and the phalaropes. These birds are associated with the margins of water or with wet ground. Most members of these families take their food, larvae, small crustacea, worms and insects, either by probing in the ooze, or by chasing it on the surface.

The larger and plumper species of wading birds were once subject to heavy shooting in many parts of the world, and still are in some places. In most areas they are now protected by law. The Eskimo Curlew had an extraordinary circular migration route from the southern tip of South America, across the Andes, north to the Arctic, and back via eastern North America. It was harassed on both trips and in its wintering areas, and may now be extinct.

The 17 species of snipe, and six species of woodcock in the world are most unlikely members of the sandpiper family of birds. Of these, several have only limited distribution on remote islands. Others are Asian, African or South American species. What concerns us here are three species, the Common Snipe, which has almost worldwide distribution, the Eurasian Woodcock, and the American Woodcock. These three may reasonably be considered game birds in the broad definition we have used in this book.

All three are heavily streaked brown birds with white markings and long bills. The snipe has much the same shape as the sandpiper, but has a somewhat heavier body and shorter legs. The Eurasian and American woodcocks are quite similar in appearance. They are squat, chunky, brown birds, with a long flat bill and a short neck. The head is large in relation to the body and the eyes are located almost at the top of the head. The American species has a plain buff breast and the Eurasian is finely barred. The tail of the former has a ruddy band near the base, ending with dark and pale bands.

Woodcocks nest in wet woodlands and brush, usually where a spring keeps the soil moist and spongy. Here they probe for food under the soil. When alarmed, they leap upward several feet and then level off in a fast erratic flight. The elaborate mating flight of these birds is exciting to watch. At dusk the male flies up in spirals until he is almost out of sight, then, after a number of circles, plunges to earth at a steep angle, zigzagging all the way, and calling with a twittering and rattling wing feathers. The final descent brings him up abruptly in a small clearing where he sits and "peents," making his derisive call. During the evening he does this time after time, and may do so again at dawn.

Snipe nest in more open ground. Its flight display is performed closer to the ground than that of the woodcock and is more erratic and swooping. It is accompanied by an eerie zooming sound caused by the vibration of tail feathers. When alarmed the snipe takes off uttering an unmistakable rasping call which sounds like pulling a boot out of soft mud.

Drainage of marshes in Europe and in the United Kingdom has reduced snipe breeding areas to such an extent that numbers are declining.

Left: American Woodcock (*Philohela minor*)   Woodcock nest in damp woods where they feed on worms which they take in wet ground with their long bills. Note that the eyes are set at the top of the head.

American Woodcock (*Philohela minor*)   This is a young bird, probably only a few days old. Woodcock hatch feathered and run about finding much of their own food when only a few hours out of the egg. This species nests in Canada and the United States.

Common Snipe (*Capella gallinago*) During the nesting season snipe do not wander far from their chosen patch of marsh. They rise with a croak when alarmed. They feed by probing in the mud and by picking up insects on the ground.

Right: Common Snipe (*Capella gallinago*) In breeding season, the Common Snipe typically executes a flight two or three hundred feet above the ground. It rolls and dives at considerable speed, rattling its outer tail feathers to make a drumming sound.

SANDGROUSE

Left: Common Snipe (*Capellu gallinago*)   The Common Snipe has an almost worldwide distribution. Northern nesting birds go far into the tundra in spring and migrate long distances to the south in the autumn.

Black-faced Sandgrouse (*Pterocles decoratus*)   Sandgrouse may nest many miles from water. In order to provide water for their young, they immerse their breasts in a pond or stream and trap the water in the feathers. They then fly back to the chicks.

The 16 members of the sandgrouse family resemble pigeons in silhouette and bone structure. It would appear that sandgrouse descend from the same stock as doves and pigeons, although some evidence indicates that they may be descendants of shorebirds. They live in dry areas of desert, savanna and bush from the southern Iberian Peninsula, throughout much of Africa, to central Asia.

Sandgrouse feed on seeds which they pick up as they run about on their short legs. They appear to prefer the dried seeds of legumes with which they fill their crops, adding grit to grind the hard seeds. They must drink every day or so and may fly up to 50 miles to reach water. They can tolerate some salt, but they are not equipped to excrete heavy saline content. Waterholes attract thousands of birds. There they stand shoulder to shoulder at the water's edge, while others wait their turn. One species, the Burchells's Sandgrouse of the Kalahari in central Africa, lands in the water and drinks while swimming.

During the breeding season sandgrouse may nest up to 50 miles from water, but usually not more than 10 or 12 miles. The young birds, usually three, of which perhaps only one will survive, are able to pick up seeds within a few hours of hatching, but will not be able to fly to water for about two months. During this period the male flies off each morning to a waterhole and, after drinking himself, saturates the feathers on his belly from which the young drink. This capability is unique to sandgrouse. The female flies away to drink first, and while she is away the male cares for the young.

Sandgrouse are primarily brown, with dark and pale streaks and spots. The head is small, the wings pointed and the body full. They range in length from 11 to 19 inches, and in weight from five to 14 ounces.

Black-faced
Sandgrouse (*Pterocles decoratus*) There are 16 species of sandgrouse. They are members of the same order of birds as pigeons and doves. All are Eastern Hemisphere species, living from eastern Europe to Japan.

139

Spotted Sandgrouse (*Pterocles senegallus*)   The Spotted Sandgrouse is
found in flatlands and hilly regions in Asia and Africa. They nest on
the ground, often in small natural depressions.

Namaqua Sandgrouse (*Pterocles namaqua*) Sandgrouse are similar in silhouette and flight to their close relatives, the pigeons and doves. This one, photographed in Namibia, is heavily spotted on the back with an attractive necklace below its grey breast.

Yellow-throated Sandgrouse (*Pterocles gutturalis*) At water holes sandgrouse congregate in flocks of thousands, but tend to feed at a considerable distance from water and in small groups. They are much subject to predation by a number of carnivores, including foxes and jackals, as well as by birds of prey.

Namaqua Sandgrouse (*Pterocles namaqua*) Sandgrouse live in arid
country where they feed on the seeds which they pick up from the
ground.

PHOTOGRAPH CREDITS

Brian Beck: 4-5, 39 top, 47, 92, 93 top, 139, 137, 141 top, 142
Fred Bruemmer: 60, 74
John Cancalosi/Valan Photos: 98 top, 100
Ron Dengler/Network Stock Photo File: 95
Victor Fazio: 126
Dr. & Mrs. Cy Hampson: 13, 43 bottom, 89, 122 bottom
Bill Ivy: 123
Edgar T. Jones: 8, 19, 22, 24, 25, 26, 27, 28, 33, 35, 37, 38, 39 bottom,
    42, 44, 45, 46, 50, 79, 98 bottom, 99, 106, 109, 115, 116, 118, 121,
    125, 127, 134, 141 bottom
Bruno Kern: 93 bottom, 101, 105
Thomas Kitchin: 54, 65, 68, 82, 86, 114, 124
Wayne Lankinen: 9, 31, 32, 34, 36, 40, 51, 62, 63, 64, 66, 67, 69, 76,
    77, 78, 87 right, 120, 129, 135
Tom & Pat Leeson: 57, 61, 72-73, 81, 136
Wayne Lynch: 20, 41, 49, 80, 88, 132
S. MacDonald: 56 and back cover
Harvey Medland/Network Stock Photo File: 83, 94
Brian Milne/First Light Associated Photographers: 58, 71
Scott Nielsen: 75
James Page: 59
George K. Peck: 17, 18, 21, 30, 48, 117, 119, 122 top, 128
Mark K. Peck: 29
Leonard Lee Rue III: front cover
Dennis W. Schmidt: 23, 55, 87 left
Duane Sept: 70
Robert C. Simpson/Valan Photos: 103, 104, 108
J.D. Taylor: 43 top, 16, 140
P. Allen Woodliffe/Network Stock Photo File: 107, 113, 133
Leonard Zorn: 2

INDEX TO PHOTOGRAPHS